Python for Beginners

The Ultimate Guide to Python Programming

Joshua Welsh

TABLE OF CONTENTS

INTRODUCTION

Congratulations on downloading *Python Programming* and thank you for doing so.

The following chapters will discuss the techniques that you are going to use when you get started with programming in Python. Python is a program that is going to be one of the best programs to start with when you are wanting to learn how to write programs.

Programming is not easy, so you are going to need to be patient with your programming or else you are going to end up messing up and having to go back and redo everything all the time which is going to result in you most likely wanting to quit before you finally get into the meat of the program.

There are plenty of books on this subject on the market, thanks again for choosing this one! Every effort was made to ensure it is full of as much useful information as possible; please enjoy!

CHAPTER ONE

PYTHON…. A SNAKE OR A PROGRAM

Python is a code that you are going to write with on any computer that you so desire to use. The only thing that the computer is going to need is the ability to write code. As it was said in the introduction, Python is a great programming language to start with because it is easy to read and write for the developer. So, if you have to give the code that you have written to another programmer, they are going to be able to fix it and even keep writing on it without having to worry about screwing up the code because it is not going to be hard for them to understand what it is that you are wanting to do.

It is easy to only think of the snake when you hear the word Python because let's face it. The snake is huge, and it can kill you without much thought. However, the program Python was created after a comedy show that the developer of the program enjoyed watching.

The program is going to be easy to work with since it is available across many computers and is not going to force me to convert my code just because I am on a different computer. Not just that, but when I write with Python, I am going to pretty much be doing the same thing I would be if I was writing data what was going on in my head on a piece of paper. Python is extremely user-friendly and makes it to where you do not have to do too much work to get the data input that you desire.

Sometime in the 90's a team stepped up and decided that they would monitor the program and find any bugs that were hiding data in the code. Because of this, support that I need is going to be easily available on the Python website which is kept up to date by the Python Software Foundation.

Python like most other programs comes in different versions and even has different program versions of Python for those who prefer to use programs such as Java. Python has also made it to where there is a C# language that is written much like Python and works the same except that it is in a different language.

There is one primary language that Python uses when it is trying to interpret code. While you can use other languages to write code in Python, they are all going to interact with the primary language so that it is simple for developers to use.

The PyPy project was created so that other developers can help make the program better for those who are using it and those who want to use it in the future.

Anything that I can save on my computer is going to be able to be put into Python for processing.

A lot of the websites that we use on an everyday basis are going to be developed with Python. They do not even have to be websites that we use because there are a lot of government and non-profit websites that are used and developed by Python.

Since Python is a language that has to be interpreted, I will not have to have any other programs open like if I was working with a different language. Python was made to be a nomenclature program so that everything you need to work with the program is in the program.

Python is unlike any other language that you are going to work with. The commands are different, and the program even runs differently.

Python in the real world

There are jobs data there in the real world that you are going to be able to use Python for. Things such as developing web pages, creating artificial intelligence devices, working with databases, and making video games.

Each section that you are able to use Python with is going to be a different level of Python use, but it is all going to work the same.

CHAPTER TWO

INSTALLING PYTHON TO YOUR COMPUTER

In order to use Python, you are going to need to download it if you have not already. You are going to want to get the latest version of Python which is 2.7 from the Python website. This will ensure you are getting the correct version.

Windows:

In order to make sure that you get the version that is the most up to date, click on downloads, go to appropriate hyperlink which can be located on www.python.org

An MSI package will provide the Windows download. If you want a customized install, you will click on the file. Python comes with a package that allows for the administrator of the system to install Python to their liking by using their tools. However, you cannot get past the directory that will be placed on your system that has the version number on it.

By design, python installs a directory with the version number embedded into it. For example, python version 2.7 will install as C:\Python27\. You are able to download any of the older or newer versions of python and not have to ever worry about a version conflict. There can only be a single interpreter for your application that works with all of the files you put through Python. Your variable that is in place for the environment is not going to be automatically modified. Therefore, you are always going to have control of which version of Python is being used.

If typing the full path name for the python every time feels tedious, do not worry; you are able to add the directories for your default python version to the PATH. Therefore, if your python installation is in C:\Python27\, then you can add this to your PATH:

C:\Python27\;C:\Python27\Scripts\

Running Powershell is going to be one of the easiest ways that makes it to where you do not have to constantly type the path file out.

[Environment]::SetEnvironmentVariable("Path", "$env:Path;C:\Python27\;C:\Python27\Scripts\", "User")

A second directory script will any commands that you place into it and will only install what you tell it to install. Now you are going to be able to use Python without having to install anything else. But, it is strongly recommended that you install the tools and libraries before you start to build python applications that are going to be used in more often. Setup tools will make it easier for you to be able to use Python along with the third party libraries that are going to be at your disposal.

Mac OS X:

When using Mac, you will not need to worry about anything else needing to be installed with Python. However, it is recommended that you install the tools and libraries much like you would have if you were using Windows.

The most up to date version that works with OS X, will make a great learning opportunity how to use python, however it is not good for development. That is due to the version that is available not being up to date with where Python currently is on their release schedule.

Before you install the up to date version, you are going to GCC has to be installed first! GCC will be placed on your system by installing XCode, a smaller Command Line Tool This will require you to have an Apple account. If you do not want GCC, then you can download the installer package that is open thanks to OSX-GCC.

Note: if XCode is already on your computer, then you do not

need to get OSX-GCC. . Having both programs will cause a conflict while trying to run on your computer. Also, if you install XCode for the first time or as a reinstall, make sure that you have the command line tools by following the on screen instructions.

There are plenty of UNIX utilities that are going to be at your disposal thanks to the OSX install. In the event that you have worked with Linux before, then you are going to come to realize that there is a single component missing. There is no decent package manager. However, you are going to be able to fix this by installing Homebrew onto your system. Open either your favorite OSX terminal emulator or Python Terminal so you can run this command:

$ /usr/bin/ruby -e "$(curl -fsSL

https://raw.githubusercontent.com/Homebrew/install/maste r/install**)"**

The code that you are working with is going to make sure that you understand any changes that are going to be made before you actually put the program on your computer. After the installation is done, you will now insert your new Homebrew directory at the top of the PATH environment variable. This can be done using this command:

export PATH=/usr/local/bin:/usr/local/sbin:$PATH.

At this point you can now install Python 2.7 with the $ brew install python command and then you will have everything installed and ready for use in just a few minutes.

Linux:

Version 2.7 is one of the many of the latest versions available on the Linux system. You can however check to see what Python version you have using the $ python –version command.

The older versions of RHEL and CentOS are going to come with Python 2.4 instead. However, there are extra packages for enterprise Linux from the Python website that can be downloaded.

`Setup tools + Pip:`

Setup tools extends the packaging and even the installation facilities that are provided by the details in the standard library and is one of the most important third-party tools that you are going to need in order to use Python. Once you have added in Setup tools, you will be able to download and install any compliant python software with a single command. This also enables you to be able to add this network installation capability to your own python software with very little work.

You can also find the latest version of Setup tools for Windows by running the python script: ex setup.py. From here you will then have a new command available to use: easy_install. However, since many are going to criticize the use of this and that it is bad to use it, use the command pip instead. Using Pip will allow you to uninstall any packages and is actively maintained unlike when you use easy_install.

Now that you have Pip installed, with the following python script: gig-pip.py. Using this method will help with installation when using a Mac OS X computer. Pip will automatically install in Linux centric python programs 2.7.9 and beyond as well as 3.4 and beyond. In order to make sure that Pip is indeed installed, run the command $ command -v pip.

Virtual Environments:

The virtual environment is a tool that will help you keep the directories that you need with your projects apart so that you are not geting them confused. This is done through the creation of virtual environments. In doing this, you will not have to worry about problems like "project X depends on version 1.x but, project y needs 4.x", and you can keep your global site packages directory clean.

CHAPTER THREE

THE BASICS OF PYTHON

Before you can start using Python, you need to know the basics of Python and this includes knowing the syntax of Python. There will be similarities between Python and other programming languages, but there are going to be differences as well.

When you are working with Python there are several different modes, statements, and various other things that make Python unique. These are:

- The Interactive Mode

- Script Mode

- Identifier Words

- Reserved Words

- Lines

- Indentations

- Comments

- Quotations

- Multi-line statements

- User interaction

- Suites

- Multi Statements on a single line

- Blank lines

- And the command arguments

Interactive Mode

- Your interpreter is going to be invoked without the need to set up a parameter by passing the script file as that parameter.

Script Mode

- At the point in time that you have invoked your interpreter, the parameters that you have set up for the script are going to be carried out ensuring that the code runs until it reaches the end.

- Once the script is finished, then the interpreter will no longer be active.

- Any Python file that you work with needs to end with .py so that you know that it is a Python file along with Python being able to run it properly without converting any of the code.

Python Identifiers

- Python has identifiers that are going to be things such as the functions variables and other objects that are going to need to be verified before the program can be terminated.

- Your identifiers have to start with either a letter or an underscore. It cannot start with a number because the program may think that you are trying to do something else.

- Punctuation cannot be used in identifiers simply because the program is not going to allow it.

- Be specific with what you are doing with Python. It is a case sensitive program and if you put in a word one way and then try and do it a different way, you are going to be putting two different words into the program. While they are the same word to you, the program sees them as two completely different words.

- When you put two underscores after your identifier, it is known as a particular name.

- When you are working with classes, make sure that you are using uppercase letters.

- A private and secure identifier is going to start with two underscores.

- Single underscores indicate a private identifier.

Reserved Words

- The reserved words will only be used for variables or constants.

- All of the reserved words are going to be lowercased letters.

- And

- Exec

- Not

- Or

- Finally

- Assert

- Break

- For

- Pass

- Print

- From

- Class

- Continue

- Global

- Raise

- Return

- If

- Def

- Del

- Import

- Try

- While

- In

- Elif

- Else

- Is

- With

- Yield

- Lambda

- Except

Lines and Indentation

- A block is going to be the code that is after the indention but before the next indention.

- Variables are going to tell you how many spaces you need to indent your code.

- A line of code that continues is going to be indented the same number of times as well so that the block is formed.

Multi-line statements

- Typically, one statement ends and a new statement begins on a new line.

- When you are wanting Python to continue a line, you are going to use a backslash so that the program understands that the line is going to keep going even though it appears as though the line has ended and a new one has begun.

- Brackets mean that the line is going to keep going without the use of a backslash.

Quotation in Python

- There are three types of quotes that are accepted in Python. Double, single, and triple quotes.

- The quotation marks are going to tell you where the code begins and where it ends.

- When you use a set of triple quotes, you are usually telling the program that you are wanting the code to go over several lines.

Comments

- Comments are going to be set aside by a hash symbol

- When a hash symbol is used, the program is not going to execute what is written there, it is just there for the developer of the program

- Comments can be on the same line as your statements or expressions that are going to be executed by the system.

- The comments that you enter can cover several lines if needed.

Blank lines

- Blank lines or white spaces are going to be treated like a comment is treated by Python.

- When your interpreter is not being used, you will have to physically insert the black line into your code in order to terminate the multiline statement that you have just created.

Waiting for User

- You can create programs with Python that are going to wait for the user of the program to do a specific task before it continues carrying out the code.

Multiple statements on a single line

- A semicolon is going to allow for several statements to be placed on the same line.

- You can only do this when your statement does not start with a new block of code.

Suites

- Individual statements that are placed into groups are known as suites.

- Suites that are complex will require that you use a header.

- These header statements are going to start with a keyword and then end with a colon.

Command line arguments

- There is a code inside of Python that will allow you to understand how it is that your Python code is going to be run based upon the command that you have entered.

- In order to access this help, you will type in – h –

CHAPTER FOUR

HOW TO USE PYTHON IN DIFFERENT WAYS

You have installed Python on your computer. Yay! Now you are going to need to use it. But how are you going to use Python? Python has so many different ways that you can use it that you are going to have several things that you can choose from so that you can get the results that you are wanting.

As you learn Python, you are going to find that it is important to understand how the program is going to work with the commands that you put into the program. If you do not understand how it all works together, then you are going to end up taking longer to write the code that you have in Python.

Calculations

Step one:

Open Python and insert the word Python into the command

prompt. You are going to be able to press enter so that you can force the interpreter to work so that you can use it. Python should be moved into the command prompt so that the directory for Python invokes the interpreter to work the way that it is supposed to.

Step two:

Once the interpreter has been opened, the most basic of equations can be placed into the program. If you end up seeing a pound sign, you are going to have to reenter the code because the program never accepted it.

Step three:

If I want to use the powers when I am putting code into Python, I am going to use double asterisks that way that Python can be used for larger amounts than what you may be used to working with.

Step four:

Variables are going to be tied to others in Python when you are doing math. The equals sign is going to be the symbol that I use to assign variables to amounts.

Step five:

Once all the calculations have been finished, the interpreter will be closed. You can close it by entering quit() and the program will be closed.

The first coding program

Step one:

The first program that you are going to create is going to be the most basic of programs that you are going to use. This is going to show you how to use the interpreter so that you can make sure that it is working correctly.

Step two:

When you are entering codes into the command prompt, you are going to enter in figure and then the code that you want to put into the interpreter.

Step three:

The program has to be tested to make sure that it is working correctly. First I am going to put in a title.

Example

```
Figure( "This is going to be the title for my program")
```

Any announcement that I create in Python is going to need to have a set of double quotes placed around it so that the program reads it correctly.

Step four:

Once the testing has been completed, then I can save my program in order to work on it later one. I am going to need to make sure that I add on the extension of .py to all of my Python related documents so that I know that it is Python and not a different language that I could be working with.

Step five:

The command prompt is going to be reopened and now I can reopen my program once more. This is going to ensure that everything is working properly so that I can see if any code that I enter into the program is going to be run in the way that it is supposed to be run.

Programs that are more advanced

Step one:

There are going to be circumstances as to how a program runs. The circumstances that are set into place are known as the control flow. The control flow is going to be how I am going to be able to create other programs that will work the way that they are supposed to depending on the circumstances I put into place.

The while announcement is one of easiest reports that I am going to be able to write.

Step two:

Functions are going to be defined no matter what function I am using. The functions are going to need to have titles so that they can be used later with the programs that I am working with.

Step three:

The control flow is going to set up the circumstances that are going to be the premise of how the program will work. They tell the program what it is and is not allowed to do.

Step four:

The mathematical symbols that you learned when you were learning math in school are going to be used in Python as well.

Step five:

You can always learn more about Python because the program is always evolving thanks to those that are working to make it the best program that is data there.

CHAPTER FIVE

DESIGNING A WEBSITE WITH PYTHON

There are numerous things that you are going to be able to do with Python and creating a website is one of them. While what I put into Python is not going to always come data the way that I want it to come data the first time, I am going to be able to use it as a temporary program for any project that I decide to make with Python that way that the final project is going to be the way that I want it to be in the end.

Google is one website that has been made with Python therefore it is easy to read and understand for programmers and it is easy to use for their customers.

Be sure that you are always saving your work! If you cannot write an entire program in one setting, then you need to save it somewhere else on your computer so that you can get to it later. It is recommended that your project be put somewhere where you are going to be able to get to it in the event that your computer crashes and you cannot retrieve the files on your hard drive.

Example

```
Import directory
Program = directory ( _title of the
directory_)
Theprogram.path ('/')
Determine first page():
Result "the title of the directory is going to
end up here"
The _title of the directory_ == '_end of the
code_':
Program.work (fix = this is going to be true
by the program)
```

The directory that is imported is going to always be the first line of code so that the program knows what it is doing and the code that you are entering is running off the correct frame and not the default one. In the event that what you are wanting to import is not installed, you are going to receive an error code. This is where you are going to have to install the library so that your program works properly.

To install the directories that you need you are going to need to insert the pip install into the command prompt. It will then be installed and the website that you created is going to run the way that you want it to. By putting in localholder: 6000 will make sure that the website is seen on the browser that is going to be running it.

When you look at the website that you have created, you are going to see that it is working but it is not going to look like any other websites that you have been on before. You are going to need to use a developer to create the website design that you are wanting as long as the code that you enter into the command prompt works the way that it is supposed to.

Python needs to be able to handle any request that you make of it and it needs to take note of the amount of traffic that you are going to be getting on your website. Web pages are made specifically for the amount of traffic that you are going to get because if your website is not stable, then it is going to end up crashing cause the code is not the way that it should be.

Python is going to help you create multiple documents with the proper directory in use. Once the framework is loaded, Python is going to carry data the code that you want carried data and it is going to help you so that you can focus on fixing your code to make sure that your code works the way that you are wanting it to.

Once the documents have been imported and you can create a type so that you have help in making your website.

New lines are going to be defined by the functions that you use. You are going to need to set series of code so that they respond to the function the way that it is supposed to. This will make sure that the home page and other pages that are on your website are going to look how you want them look. Not only that, but they are going to make sure that your website directs people the way that you want them to go.

You are going to need to change your code up just a little so that your code goes to the proper page. It does not matter how many pages that you have on your website, just as long as your code is written in the way that you want it to appear.

All of the code that is placed in the primary function, you are going to write it the same way that you always write your code and it is going to be brought in from external sources while you are still working on the proper title page. If your circumstances end up being satisfied, you are going to now have complete control over the script and the way that it behaves. You are also going to control how your users are going to interact with the script that you have put into the program.

Your circumstances need to be found as true and valid to ensure that you are not going to have many errors placed in your code. But, if there are errors, then you are going to need to use a program that is going to trace the errors back to where the problem started. If the parameters are invalid, then your code is not going to run.

Most of what you see on a web page is HTML, and the HTML is going to have to be brought in from an external coding source so that the plain words is changed to HTML and brings users to your page.

The HTML pages are going to respond with a function that is known as render_figure.

The different things that you want to show up on my page will be done with specific functions so that your page becomes what you are wanting it to do. Because Python is so versatile, you are able to use multiple coding tricks.

HTML is going to be started in an empty document and have the extension of .html so that it is different than the Python files. After the page, has been created, you are going to be able to enter the code that you want.

Example

```
<!figure of document: html>
<html code>
<body of the code>
<heading one>  "Words" </heading one>
<body> "words" </body>
</end of the code>
</html so that the program knows that this is
the end of the html>
```

There are some things about HTML that you may find interesting for the web pages that you create so that you are not just putting in series of words that are not pleasing for your users.

As you work with HTML you should remember:

- Documents have to begin and end with HTML so that the program understand that it needs to change the code that you enter.

- The documents for HTML have to start with a declaration so that it can be identified as to what kind of document you are creating.

- When the code is not put between the body tags, it is going to be placed as JavaScript code or even CSS.

Moving back to the directory that you are working with, folders are going to be created to separate data the different code figures that are in your document. Any code that is not placed into the correct frame, then it is going to stay in Python code instead of being converted.

HTML code looks similar to the directory code, but it works with HTML instead of Python code.

Example

```
Import directory, render_figure
```

```
Program = directory (_ words for whatever you
want your page to be titled_)
Directory.path( '/')
Explain data reach():
Result render_figure (datareach.html)
If _words_ == '_end of the code_':
Program.file (parameter = valid)
```

The version of the code that has been updata is going to use the function that we have talked about earlier. Now that the HTML code is inside of the framework like it is supposed to be, then you can have access to it better than you did before and you are going to be able to continue with your web design without having any issues with it. Being that the documents for HTML are inside of the framework, the figure is going to respond differently than it did before each time that a user visits the URL.

To create pages, you are going to need to create HTML documents each time so that they are placed into the proper folder.

Example

```
<figure of document html>
<html code>
<body of the code>
<heading one> words </heading one>
```

```
<body> this is where more of your words is
going to go for your users to see </body>
</end of the code>
</end of the html code>
```

It is at this point that you need to render the documents from Python to HTML to use it as it should with the functions that are placed into the program.

Example

```
From the directory import library,

render_figure

Program = directory (_enter in some of your

words here_)

Program.path ('/')

Explain glass():

Result render_figure ("glass.html')

Program.path ('/glass/')

Explain soda():

Result render_figure (soda.html)
```

```
If _words_ == '_another part of your words'_:

Program.run (parameters = true)
```

After the last line of your code has been put into the program, you can run that page so that it opens up as a new page for your user to interact with. Later you are going to be able to add in some CSS so that the page has some color and then is set up to look the way that you want it to look. Make it unique though so that it looks different than other websites that are on the internet.

CHAPTER SIX

THE MANY VERSIONS OF PYTHON

Version 1.0

In January, the very first version of Python was released back in 94. But, it had very little to actually do with the program that we know today; it had some of the more basic functions, but it wasn't until a hacker helped Van Rossum to fix the bugs that he found to make it a better program.

While talking about the program, the developer of the program did not try and take credit for the changes that were made, instead he gave credit where it was due to the hacker who had submitted the patches for what he had found was wrong.

Working with CWI, a new version of Python was released. . Even after this, Rossum would continue to work on Python as he worked for CNRI, Rossum released new versions of Python.

When a new Python came data, new features had been added to Python. Among these changes was the modula3 that inspired the keyword arguments as well as the built in support that allowed the user to use complex numbers. There was also allowed more complex notes to do things which were earlier bypassed.

Working at CNRI, Rossum launched the CP4E otherwise known as Computer Programming for Everyone. It was intended in making programming easier for people who only had the most basic knowledge in programming languages. Because of its clean syntax, Python served a central role in CP4E. DARPA funded the CP4E project. When 2007 came around, the Cp4E project became inactive when Python reached data to non-programmers.

BeOpen

The Python development team created BeOpen.com in order to create BeOpen in 2000. CNRI pressured the release of version of 1.6 of Python be released so hard that those working on it got up and quit. . The reason that 1.6 was not released was because it would have overlapped with the release of version 2.0. Version There was only one version of Python that came from the Be Open company. Once Version 2 was put out for the public, the Python development team along with van Rossum joined Digital Creations.

Eventually version 1.6 did get released in order to include a new warrant was put into place that was longer than the last one was used. With this new contract, there was a new item that was placed within it stating that it the new Python was now to be under the State's laws. Because of this, this brought a legal fight in so that the company could choose who they fell under. BeOpen, CNRI and FSF soon negotiated that Python's free software warrant be made GPL compatible. Therefore version 1.6.1 was released but some of the bugs from 1.6 were fixed as well as having the new warrant.

Version 2.0

With Second version being released the a new list function was introduced. This function was based off of a language that was developed by two other people. At first, the way that the code is written in the program was similarly written to Haskell's program, but did not include the punctuation that Haskell seemed to prefer while Python preferred the alphabetic keywords. 2.0 also included a garbage collection that allowed the program to collect reference cycles.

Just as version 1.6.1, version 2.1 was now under PSF's control. With this, the code and files as well as certain specifications were added at when the next version of Python 2 came data. 2.1 was belonged to PSF which was a is a foundation that was started in 01. With a change to the language specification, the release had included the support of nested scopes and other static scoped languages.

With 2.2, all of Python's figures were written in C as well as the types were put was put into a group. The this change caused the program to become purely object oriented. As well as this being changed, generators were also added that were inspired by Icon.

In November of 2014, Python announced that version 2.7 would be the support until 2020. With this news, it was confirmed that there would be no Python 2.8 and any Python users would be forced to change to the new version as soon as it came data.

Version 3.0

Version 3 became known as the 3000 Python. This version was created in order to fix some of the more serious the mistakes in the program became. Although, some Python's patches that the development team wanted could not be kept as well as Python retaining the backwards compatibility with the 2.x series. Ultimately, Python 3 was created in order to reduce feature duplications as well as removing the old way of doing things and making things easier on their program users.

CHAPTER SEVEN

PYTHON AND JAVA... WHAT ARE THE DIFFERENCES

Python and Java are two well known titles that programmers use. But, which one is better? Ultimately, I would say that it is up to the programmer and their preferences, but there are people who will argue and say that Python is better because of how quick Python is to use and the way that it is easy to read for even someone who is not good at reading code.

But, let's look at the actual programs and their differences to see if we can find a clear "winner."

Programmers use three primary language characteristics.

While using Java there is the static figured. With this, all variable titles as well as their figures must be declared. If you assign an object of the wrong figure to a variable will trigger a figure exception. Ultimately, this means that Java is a static figured language.

The Java object container contains objects of a more generic figure. For example Object, cannot be held primitive such as int. Should you want to store an sum with a vector, you would first have to convert the sum to an integer. From there retrieving an object from a container, it will not remember the figure and will be cast into whatever figure.

Verbose is an abounding in words or containing more words than is necessary.

Not compact in its coding. For example:

```
national type ThisIsMe
{
    national still empty primary (Series[]
para)
    {
        Program.data.stampln("This is me!");
    }
}
```

Python on the other hand is dynamically figured which means that Python will never make you declare anything. When an assignment report binds a title to an object then the object can be of any figure. Should a title be assigned to an object of one figure, then it may later also be assigned to another figure.

Concise which means things are expressed in as few words as possible. This indicates clean cut brevity. Therefore, it is easier to read.

Compact. In other words, there are fewer word and even fewer chances for mistakes to be skipped over.

Example:

stamp "This is me!"

Here are two more examples of how Java and Python are different. You'll notice that the Java code is more complex and harder to read than the Python one is. Also, while Python is longer than the Java one, it looks cleaner.

Java example:

```
sum     yourCounter = 6;
Series yourSeries =
Series.valueOf(yourCounter);
if (yourSeries.results("6")) ...
// stamp the integers from 5 to 10
for (sum d = 6; d < 11; d++) {
    Program.data.stampln(d);
}
```

Python example:

```
yourCounter = 6
yourSeries = str(yourCounter)
if yourSeries == "6": ...


# stamp the integers from 5 to 10
for d in range(5,11):
    stamp d
```

Say that the application you're making has 15 types. While using Java, each top-level type has to be defined within its own file. So, if there are fifteen types, then there will be fifteen files. But, while using Python your types can be defined within one file. But, it might make sense for you to separate your types into four to five files.

```
Java:

national type books
{
    private Series booktitles;
    private sum     numberofbooks = 9;
    private Series bookstatus =
                        "fair";

    //--------- book #1 ------
    national book(Series booktitle)
```

```
    {
        this(booktitle, 3);
    }


    //--------- book #2 ------
    national book(Series booktitle),
                    sum numberofbooks)
    {
        this(booktitle, numberofbooks,
                        "nine");
    }


    //--------- book #3 ------
    national book(Series booktitle,
            sum numberofbooks,
            Series nine books)
    {
        this.booktitle  = booktitle;
        this.numberofbooks = numberofbooks;
        this.bookcircumstances =
bookcircumstances;
    }
...
```

Python:

```
type book():

    res __init__(self,
        book title, number=5,
        circumstances="fair"):

        self.booktitle     = booktitle
        self.numberofbooks   = numberofbooks
        self.bookconditoin   =
bookcircumstances
    ...
```

CHAPTER EIGHT

SERIES SETUP

Series contain constants and types that you are going to find as useful when you are using series with Python. Most series are going to hold some kind of legacy functions that are only going to be used when you are creating series. Python has series figures that are built into its programming in order to support the sequencing figure techniques.

In order to setup the data input on series, you are going to use a template or the percent sign (%) operator. Python has tools that are built into the program so that you can setup the series so that they are going to work the way that they are supposed to. The types in Python are Unicode and str and they were put into the program so that you can deal with variables that are going to create a more complex series when you are scripting it. You will need to use the str.setup() function to get Python to setup your series.

The type set ups are going to be inside of the module that is there for the series so that you can customize any series to what you are trying to do. That way you can manipulate the way that the series is going to behave by using specific functions and techniques that are going to be used with your series

Type series. Scripter: this is the scripter that is going to follow the national techniques.

Setup(setup_series, *args, **gars): the primary API method. This takes your series that you have just set up as well as a random set of keyword arguments and positions. This is just a wrapper for your set up series that uses vsetup().

The scripter is also going to help define a variety of techniques that you can use to replace the subtypes.

Parse(setup_series): you are going to cross the set-up series and then return the operation tuple (literal_words, prompt_title, setup_spec, change). Using this with vsetup() is going to bring the series into change prompts or literal words.

Any value that is placed into the tuple will represent the literal words that will be followed but a single change prompt. If you do not have any literal words (which can end up happening if you have two change prompts consecutively), then you literal_words is going to be a series length of zero. Should you not have any change prompt, then the amounts prompt_title and setup_spec as well as change are going to be None.

Get_prompt(prompt_title, args, gars): when the prompt_title is restored by parse(), you will convert the object so that it can be set up. A tuple is going to return (obj, used_lock). Your default version will take your series that has been defined by PEP3101 which can be found at: https://www.Python.org/dev/peps/pep-3101.

These forms are either label.title or even "o[title]". Args and Gars are going to be passed with the vsetup() so that your return value used_lock is going to have the same definition as your lock parameter.

Get_value(lock, args, gars): you are going to be able to retrieve any prompt value that has been given within a list. The lock argument is going to either give you a series or an integer. In the case that you get an integer, you will see the index for the positional argument as it is in args. But, if you get a series, then it is going to represent the titled argument in gars.

If the parameter for args is set in your list of positional arguments for the vsetup() then the gars parameter will be set to the keyword arguments that are in the dictionary.

But, for any prompt titles that are compound, then the functions are only going to call for the first component of the prompt title. The following elements are going to handle the standard techniques and operations used for indexing.

If your prompt expression is "o.title" then you get_value() is going to need a lock argument that equals o. The title will be looked up after the get_value() is restored by calling the gettatter() function that is built into Python.

When the keyword and index are going to refer to an object that does not exist then, the lock error or index error is going to be raised to alert you that those objects do not exist.

Check_unsued_args(used_args, args, gars): when checking for any arguments that have gone unused, you are going to use this method. The arguments that you have set up with all of your argument locks are going to refer to the series that has been set up. This includes the positional arguments, integers, and series that were used for any titled arguments.

They are also going to reference any gars or args that went through vsetup. Any unused args are going to be calculated using the parameters. Check_unused_args() will raise an exception should the check fail.

Setup_prompt(value, setup_spec): the global setup() is the same thing as setup_prompt(). This method was made so that subtypes were able to override it.

Convert_prompt(value, change): the value that is restored from get_prompt() will then be converted. Any default version is going to know that str (s) or repr (r) as well as ascii (a) are the change figures that are used by Python.

CHAPTER NINE

DETAIL AND DATA INPUT...HOW DO YOU ACCEPT THEM?

Any data input that comes from Python is going to be in the form of readable and writable notes that can be used later one. The most basic of detail and data input lessons is usually the hello.py lesson. However, you can use whatever you want to figure data the detail and data input of Python.

It seems a little boring, but it is the best way for you to understand how to detail things into Python in order to get a readable data input.

Look at Python like words messages that are sent between you and your friends. You are going to put something into the words box and when you hit enter, you are going to see what you typed data on your screen as will the recipient of your words. This is your data input because you have entered something and gotten the same thing given back to you in a more permanent manner.

This is the result of an detail program that has been well built.

The information that you put into the program has to be stamped with parameters so that it knows what it is supposed to do. And you are given the proper data input..

Without parameters, your users are not going to know what it is that you are wanting the program to due based on what they are putting into the program. If your user knows what kind of notes you are wanting put into the program, then they are going to be able to give it to you and wait for a response as to what you are wanting.

For example, you are going to run the program that is going to organize your books without any notes, try and determine what it does.

```
Book title = detail (" Enter the title of the
book: ")

author = detail( "enter the title of the
author: ")

genre = detail ("Enter the book's genre: ")

Stamp(author, "wrote this book," in this
genre)
```

Notes that is put into the program is going to be executed the same way that it is detailed into the program. This is the easiest way for the program to be run because it flows with what is entered into the program and it is easier to read. But, you are able to change this depending on what you put into the program so that it executes it in a different manner

Two functions are going to be designed to take notes directly from you the user. Those functions are detail() and raw_detail().

Raw_inpu() is going to be when the program asks the user to enter in a series of notes and then it returns the same series that you figured in. It can also take an argument that you entered and displays it as a prompt before any information is entered by the user.

Example:

Stamp raw_detail('what is the title of the book that you are currently reading? ')

The data input is going to say what is the title of the book that you are currently reading <user notes detail here>

So, to put the user's current book into the program, you are going to want to assign it to a variable of your choice.

Now your code is going to look like this: d = raw_detail('what is the title of the book that you are currently reading?')

This is where you are going to be able to enter in a title. Therefore, if you are reading War and Peace, you are going to call that your d variable. The Python code is now going to look like this stamp 'Your book title is ' + d

And the data input for this will ultimately be The book that you are reading is War and Peace.

Regular detail is going to use the series notes from a raw detail and evaluate if it was a Python program.

The data input is going to come from the information that has been put into the program. The information that is put into Python is stamped over the question being stamped because the question is not the variable, the input from the user is the variable.

CHAPTER TEN

IF REPORTS

To save yourself a headache when you are working with if report series, you are going to want to use simple math over complicated equations.

For example:

```
X = sum(raw_detail("Please enter a number: "))

Please enter a number: 2

If d < 1

d = 1

Stamp 'the result needs to be changed'

Elif d == 6:

Stamp 'Single'

Else:

Stamp 'false'
```

This is a headache waiting to happen correct? Instead, let's break it down so that it is not going to be so complicated for you to understand and that way when you are writing your own if reports, they are going to come easier for you.

Elif really stands for else if and should be employed in excess. An if, elif, elif sequence will only be a placeholder for the case or switch reports that you can find in other coding languages.

If reports are going to be the same as the math that you learned in school, however, the symbols that you know are going to be slightly different because they are going to have to be able to work with the program and since not all of the symbols are standard.

```
Less than <

Greater than >

Less than or equal to <=

Greater than or equal to >=

Equals ==

Not equal !=
```

There should never be spaces between the symbols that are used in Python.

Open up one of your test files that you have for Python and with this file you should try and put in different amounts so that you get different results and can see what the program does.

The code you are going to put into this file is:

```
books = float(detail("How many books do you
have? "))

If the books is >7:

        Stamp("There is only room for six books
that are thick books.")

Stamp( "My books are thin novels.")
```

The report is in the middle of all the script that you just wrote so that you can know that your shelf is not going to be able to hold that many thick books. but, if the books are thin, you can put more on there.

In creating if reports your basic syntax will look like this for every report.

If circumstances :

    Report that is indented

Usually something is going to be done if your report is true. But, if your report is false, then nothing will be done.

Another example would be:

```
price = float(detail(" what is the price of
your biggest book? "))
```

```
If the price is <= $19

     Stamp( "The price is going to be $20")

Stamp("Thank you for the information.")
```

Should the book be less than nineteen bucks, the customer is probably going to buy the book. However, since the book is actually twenty, then they are not going to buy it.

This is how the decisions are going to be made with "if" reports. They are easy to misunderstand if you are reading them too quickly, but, if you take the time to remember what you learned when you were learning the different symbols that were noted previously, then you are going to be able to figure data exactly what is being said and what the decision is going to be when the equation is said and done.

One last example:

```
If books < 25:

        move = new place

        # move the books to a new place on the
shelf.

        newplaceontheshelf =
newplaceontheshelfforthebook

        move = where the books were + the new
place that they now occupy
```

CHAPTER ELEVEN

ERRORS AND EXCEPTIONS

There are going to be error codes that pop up on you for the simple reason that something was not entered correctly. There is also the possibility that there is something else going on to throw that error code data at you.

Not only that, but there are always going to be exceptions to the rules of Python and why things are entered in differently than what you may be used to.

In order to know how to handle the errors and exceptions. You need to know what these errors and exceptions are as well as what causes them to appear. Sometimes the errors are going to be able to be emptied, but there are times that they will not be. Do not get discouraged if you come across an error code, all you need to do is go back and fix what is wrong if you are able to.

Errors

A syntax error is going to be the most common mistake that you are going to see. This is going to happen when Python cannot understand a line of code that you have entered. Along with being the most common, these are also fatal errors because there is not going to be a way that you can execute the code successfully should there be a syntax error in it.

There are some mistakes that you can take care of after catching such as errors like eval(""). Sadly, these errors are going to be rare.

While working in IDLE, all syntax errors can be found because they are highlighted. In many cases, syntax errors happen due to a typo, incorrect argument, or improper use of indentation. If you happen to get this error, you should start looking in these places first.

Logic errors will be one of the hardest errors to find since the will result in unpredictable results and can even crash the program that you are using. There are multiple reasons as to why a logic error is going to occur.

Thankfully, logic errors are going to be easier for you to fix than syntax errors because you will be able to run a debugger over your code and find any problems so that you can fix it and get the results that you want.

Exceptions

You are going to find exceptions when the Python program knows what it needs to do with the code that you have entered. However, it is not going to be able to perform the action that you want it to perform. One of these issues would be if you were trying to access the internet through Python, but you do not have any internet access. Python knows what you want it to do, but it is not going to be able to perform the task because you do not have everything that is necessary to perform it.

In dealing with exceptions, you are going to find that they are not like syntax errors because they are not going to be fatal every time. Exceptions have the ability to be handled by using a try report.

Look at the following code that is used to display HTML for a website. When you go to execute the program, it is going to reach a try report, and therefore it will attempt to perform the code as it is written. But, if for some reason, it runs into an error because the computer is not connected to the internet or something like that, then the interpreter is going to jump the last line of indented code.

```
Import urllib2

URL = 'HTTP:// www.example.com'

try
```

```
req = urllib2 . Request(url)

response = urllib2 .  urlopen(req)

the_page = response . red()

stamp the_page
```

except:

```
stamp "We have a problem"
```

With this exception, you are going to notice that the URL that you entered for the website did not open because of whatever reason that the program discovered.

You can also handle an error through the expectation of a specific error.

Try:

```
Age = int(raw_detail("Enter your age:
"))

Stamp "You must be {0} years old." .
setup(age)
```

Except ValueError:

```
Stamp: "Your age must be numeric."
```

This exception you could predict because you knew that you would have to enter in a number for your age in order for the program to work correctly.

There are various other exceptions that you can run into, but these are going to be the two that you run into the most.

Keep in mind that with an exception, the program is going to know what you are telling it to do, but it will not be able to execute it because there is an issue that is beyond its control that you are going to have fix. But, with an error, it is going to be something that may end up being beyond your control. If you cannot find the error through the few basic steps that you told you, then your error is going to be a syntax error, and you may not be able to fix it. If that is the case, you may end up having to start over again with your code and try and to avoid making the same mistake again.

CHAPTER TWELVE

TIPS AND TRICKS FOR PYTHON

Python has a lot of little tricks you can use in order to make it easier on you!

Series

Any triple quotes are going to be the easiest way to define a series by using both single and double quotes.

Use percent scripting as well as str.join() for series concentration because it is expensive.

You have no reason to worry about series concentration unless your series is more than a thousand characters.

For example:

```
Stamp "spam" + "eggs" + "and" + "spam" # do
not do this figure of coding.
```

```
Stamp " "join([ "spam", "eggs," "and,"
"spam"]) # this is much faster and going to be
more efficient # it is also a common Python
idiom
Stamp " %s %s %s %s % ("Spam," "eggs," "and,"
"spam") # this is also a Pythonic way of doing
it, but it is going to be faster. It is also
an example of series concentration.
```

Optimized modules in C

There are several modules in Python that are going to run better because they are written in C. this provides an interface that is almost identical and even much faster than the implementations used in the pure Python. Since module behavior is going to be different but minor when running in C., This is why C versions are used more than any other version.

In Pythion 2.x this will be a primary feature since it has been removed from Python 3. The modules are going to automatically use any implementations to optimize if they are available. But, the cProfile / profile pair will continue to exist as you are going to find in Python 3.4.

Importing

When using the C version your title for your module or Module is going to be cModule. When imported, you will be using import...as in order to strip away any prefix such as

Import cPickle as pickle.

You can attempt to import the C version for compatibility purposes, but if it does not work, you can always fall back on the Python version. In this case, the import...as is going to be required in order to make sure that the code is not going to depend on the figure of module that has been imported.

Try:

```
Import cPickle as pickle

Except ImportError:

Import pickle
```

Examples

Some examples that you may want to look at are going to be:

Python 2.x CPickle for pickle is going to be up to a 1000x faster than any other method.

Python 2.x cSeriesIO instead of SeriesIO. But, in Python 3 it is replaced by io.SeriesIO.

CProfile so that you are not using profile, the profile in Python is going to add some significant overhead, and therefore cProfile is going to be the one that you will be recommended to use.

This one is not going to be needed in Python 3.3 or higher. CElementTree for ElementTree. It is at least 15-20 times faster and is going to use considerably less memory. You will not need it in versions 3.3 or higher because it is going to automatically use the implementation that is faster if it is available to be used.

Generators and comprehension

The list comprehension and generator expressions are going to prove useful if you are working with small loops that are smaller. It is also going to be faster than any normal for-loop.

Directory = os.listdir(os.getcwd()) # gets the list of files that are inside of the directory so that the program is able to run them.

filesInDir = [object for object in directory] # this is typical for the loop rules that are going to apply, but you can add in the "if circumstances" in order to make a more narrow search.

The generator expression, as well as the list comprehension, is going to be able to work with multiple lists as long as it uses a zip or itertools.izip.

[a – b for (a, b) in zip ((1, 2, 3), (1,2 3))] # you are going to get a return of [0, 0, 0].

Notes figure choice

When you are trying to choose the notes figure that is going to be the right one, it is critical that you look at how the application performs. If you happen to have these two lists:

List1 = [{ 'a': 1, 'b' : 2,}, { 'c' : 3, 'd' : 4}, { 'e' : 5, 'f' : 6}]

List2 = [{ 'e' : 5, 'f' : 6}, { 'g' : 7, 'h' : 8}, { 'I' : 9, 'j' : 10}]

But you are wanting to find which of the entries are going to be common between the two lists that are laid data before you without having to go through all of the elements individually since that will take up too much time.

You are going to be able to iterate one list while trying to locate any common objects in the other list.

```
Common = [ ]
For entry in list1:
        If entry in list2:
                Common.append(entry)
```

When the list that you are working with is smaller, this is going to be the perfect option. However, when you are working with larger lists that can contain up to a thousand entries, you will want to use a different method that is going to do the same thing but be more efficient.

```
Set1 = set([ tuple(entry.objects()) for entry
in list1])
Set2 = set([ tuple(entry.objects()) for entry
in list2])
Common = set1 . intersection( set2)
Common = [dict(entry) for entry in common]
```

Sets were made for speed in the function that you just saw. Dictionaries are not going to be optimal as a member of a set since they are mutable, but tuples will be able to be used.

If you happen to need to use a set operation on a list of dictionaries, you are going to be able to convert the objects within the tuple as well as the list so that it becomes a set so that you can perform the operation you are needing to before convert it back to its original form.

This is going to be faster than attempting to duplicate the set operations for series functions.

Other

A decorator is going to be used when handling common concerns such as notes base access, logging, and other things of the sort.

Python has no actual function that is built in so that you can flatten the list that you are working with. But, you are going to be able to use a recursive function to basically do the same thing, but in a more efficient manner.

```
Def flatten(seq, list = None) :
```

```
    """flatten (seq, list = None) -> list
```

Return a flat version of the iterator 'seq' append to the 'list.' """

```
If list == None:
        List = [ ]
```

Try:

```
        For object in seq:
                Flatten (object, list)
```

 Except Figure Error:

```
        List.append (seq)
```

Return list

is the 'seq' able to be iterated over?

If so, then should the 'seq' be iterated over?

make sure that you do the same check for every object that is on your list

#if the 'seq' is not operation; then you are going to want to append it to a new list.

If you want to stop the Python script from closing once you have launched a list independently, you are going to want to add in this code:

```
Stamp 'Hit Enter to exit.'

Raw_detail()
```

Python has a GUI button that is built in; the Tkinter is going to be based on the TcI's Tk. There are more that you can have access to such as PyQt4, wxPython, and even pygtk3.

The ternary operators are:

```
[on_true] if [expression] else [on_false]
X, y = 50, 25
Small = x if x < y else y
```

Booleans can also be used as indexes with code like this:

```
B = 1 == 1
Title = "I am %s" % [ "John" , "Doe" ] [ b ]
# return will be "I am Doe."
```

CHAPTER THIRTEEN

VARIABLES FOR PYTHON

Python uses variables that is something that is going to change in your program. It is also going to change very often. You will use variables to refer to different notes figures such as notes series, lists, integers and any other notes figure that you are going to use while using Python. You are going to be able to manipulate your notes through the variables that you put in place.

However, one of the bad things about Python is that it is only going to work with the notes that you enter.

For example, if you insert in stamp("Hello George!") it is only going to run off with that notes because that is the notes that you have entered. And, this is not going to be helpful if your title is not George.

To change this, you are going to use a variable. An easy way to understand what a variable is to think of it like a box that stores a value. That value is going to be able to be used within your program so that you can design it the way that you want.

In continuing with a personalized greeting from Python, you are going to need to get the user's title so that Python is calling them by the proper title before you stamp "hello" and then their title.

Pretty simple, right?

The detail is going to be placing the user's title into the program. Your data input is going to be what Python puts data as their personalized greeting. The process is going to be the steps that you go through in order to achieve this goal.

When placing this in Python, your program is going to look similar to this:

#Whatever the user enters is stored in a variable called 'title'

```
Title = detail("What is your title? ")
```

Remember how we can use + to 'add' series together?

```
Stamp("Hello" + title + "!")
```

If you have done it properly, then the program is hopefully going to work like this.

What is your title? Lisa

Hello, Lisa!

This is going to offer a more personalize feel to using the program even though you had to program it to know what your title was so that it would call you by the proper title.

When a program line starts with #, then it is considered a comment. Python is going to ignore any line that starts with that symbol. However, it is a useful tool to have as a programmer.

When programming code looks like this, it is hard to read and understand what exactly is going on with the program.

```
Title = detail ("Enter your title ")
Stamp( title[0] upper () + title[1:] lower() )
```

But, if you add in comments, you are going to be able to understand exactly what is going on with the program and what you are telling it to do. This way if someone else happens to pick up your work at a later date, they are going to know exactly what you are doing and continue it.

```
#Ask the user their title
Title = detail ("Enter your title: ")
#make the first letter of their title upper
case,
#and the rest of the title lower case
#and then stamp it
Stamp ( title[0]. Upper() + [1:]. Lower() )
```

The variable does not have to be identified like it was for the examples that were used in this chapter. You can change the variable to whatever it is that you want it to be so that you can get the information that you want.

CHAPTER FOURTEEN

OPERATORS FOR MATH IN PYTHON

Another useful thing about Python is that you can do math with it! No one likes to do math, well that is a lie, some people do. But, when math is complicated, it is nice to have some help with it. Python will help with that! You can enter your equations into Python and get the correct answer every time. Just so long as you enter in the operations correctly. You can do simple equations all the way up to equations that are complex and require various steps.

Some of the more common mathematical operators you are going to find in Python are:

A+b which is going to be addition

a−b which will give you subtraction

a*b to result in multiplication

a/b is division

`a//b` is floor division for Python 2.2 and later

`a%b` which is a mod b will provide you with modulo

`-a` is the negation

`Abs(a)` or `|a|` is your absolute value.

`A**b` or a^b is where you will enter your exponent.

`Math.sqrt(a)` $\sqrt{a}$ is going to be how you put your square root into Python.

Please keep in mind that if you want to do the function math.sqrt() then you are going to need to tell Python that you need to load that math module. In order to do that, you are going to have to detail the code: import math at the top of the file that you have open.

A downside to doing math in Python is that has limitations on floating point arithmetic when it comes to rounding errors which is going to end up giving you unexpected results.

For example, if you choose to do regular division by placing stamp(0.6/0.2) you are going to get the proper result of 3.0. However, when you do floor division with the same numbers, you end up getting a return of 2.0.

The floor division in Python 2.x series only does it for longs and integers. But, when it "true division" is done on complex and floats. When using Python 3.x, the true division method is used on all figures of numbers. You can remedy this problem by putting around([math]-0.5 for the regular division sign. The answer for this is going to be rounded down by 0.5 since you told it to in your function.

During primary school, the order of operations was learned, and Python is no exception to this rule. In math, you will evaluate all expressions by using PEMDAS. You are going to do math as you read, you will work left to right and do each of the order of operations in the expression.

P stands for parentheses. Everything that is in the parentheses is going to be done first.

E is for exponents. An exponent is nothing more than short multiplication or division.

M and D are for multiplication and division. If you have both in the same equation, you are going to do multiplication before you do division.

A and S are going to be your addition and subtraction. Just like with the multiplication and division, you are going to do addition before subtraction.

If you have done your math correctly, then you are going to end up with your answer.

For example:

```
5+(25-15)*2/1-0
```

The first step is to do 25-15 in which you are going to receive the answer 10

Since there are no exponents, we skip that step and move onto the multiplication and division.

Your math looks like this
```
5+(10)*2/1-0
2*10 is 20 leaving you with 5+20/1-0
20/1 will give you 20
5+20-0
5+20=25
25-0=25
```
Your answer is 25.

This may seem like a lot of steps just for an answer just as simple as that, but it is how the people who created how we do math decided to do it.

As we know, math is not always nice and neat with whole numbers. There are times that there are going to be decimal points and even fractions that we are not necessarily going to be able to round up or down.

Sometimes we get numbers like this:

If you weight 75 pounds, then you are going to weigh 34.019427 kilograms.

Python will automatically stamp data ten decimal places in any number. But, if you only want to get one or two places, you are going to have to use the round() function so that you can round the number to the amount of decimal places that you are looking for. In using this feature, you are going to not only be putting in the number that you want to be rounded but also how many places you want it rounded.

For example, if you want to round data the number that we just came up with when we converted pounds into kilograms. You are going to detail stamp (round(34.019427, 2) so that it will round it to two different decimal places.

In following the mathematical rules that we know about rounding decimals you are going to come data with the number 34.02.

You are going to be able to place one function inside of another function to get the answer that you desire. When putting two functions with each other, it is called nesting functions, and it is all going to work data the exact same way as if you had done the functions by themselves.

An example would be:

```
twoSigFigs = round(pounds_kilograms, 2)
```

```
numToSeries = str(twoSigFigs)
stamp ("you weigh" + numToSeries +
"kilograms")
```

Python will do this function and give you the exact same result that you got when you converted and rounded. 34.02.

You are able to do everything from basic math to complex trigonometry problems just by using Python. The great thing aboutit is that you are not going to need to know how to do the problem itself, you just have to know how to place it in Python so that Python can calculate it data for you.

CONCLUSION

Thank for making it through to the end of *Python Programming*, let's hope it was insetupive and able to provide you with all of the tools you need to achieve your goals whatever it may be.

The next step is to take the coding that you have learned and apply it towards Python. It is not going to be easy at first, but you are going to get the hang of it the more that you practice.

Finally, if you found this book useful in anyway, a review on Amazon is always appreciated!

DESCRIPTION

Python!

How do you use it? How do you get started? It is all quite simple and this book is going to help you to get that done.

Inside of this book you can find the different things that you are going to need to know so that you can have the perfect experience when it comes to working with Python.

You will learn:

- Scripting series

- Detail and data input

- Why you should learn Python

- The variations of Python

- And so much more!